Quotation Quizzlers

Puzzling your way through famous quotations

Written by: *Philip A. Steinbacher* ▼ Illustrated by: *Stephanie O'Shaughnessy*

Routledge
Taylor & Francis Group

NEW YORK AND LONDON

First published 2005 by Prufrock Press Inc.

Published 2021 by Routledge
605 Third Avenue, New York, NY 10017
2 Park Square, Milton Park, Abingdon, Oxon OX14 4RN

Routledge is an imprint of the Taylor & Francis Group, an informa business

ISBN 13: 978-1-59363-101-7 (pbk)

Edited by Dianne Draze and Sonsie Conroy

Contents

Sample Quizzler

This is a quotation quizzler. It is a puzzle that contains a quote from a famous person. The letters in the large boxes at the bottom of each column can be placed in the spaces in the top portion of the grid. When the letters are unscrambled and placed in the correct order, they will spell out the words of the quote.

							!
M **O** **L**	**R** **I** **E** **G**	**B** **I**	**D** **E** **V** **G**	**E** **R** **I** **E**	**V** **A** **T**	**T** **Y** **M** **E**	**H** **E**

What is the quote?

_____

_____

_____

4

Sample Solution

1. Begin with the blank quotation quizzler.

							!
M	R	B	D	E	V	T	H
O	I		E	R	A	Y	E
L	E	I	V	I	T	M	
G			G	E		E	

2. As you place the letters in the boxes, cross out the letters you have used. Begin by looking at the columns with the fewest letters to place. Look for arrangements of letters that will spell words.

			g	i	v	e	
m	e						!
~~M~~	R	B	D	E	~~V~~	T	H
O	I		E	R	A	Y	E
L	~~E~~	I	V	~~I~~	T	M	
	G		G	E		~~E~~	

3. When all of the letters are correctly placed, they spell out a quote by a famous person.

	G	i	v	e		m	e
l	i	b	e	r	t	y	
o	r		g	i	v	e	
m	e		d	e	a	t	h!
~~M~~	~~R~~	~~B~~	~~D~~	~~E~~	~~V~~	~~T~~	~~H~~
~~O~~	~~I~~		~~E~~	~~R~~	~~A~~	~~Y~~	~~E~~
~~L~~	~~E~~	~~I~~	~~V~~	~~I~~	~~T~~	~~M~~	
	~~G~~		~~G~~	~~E~~		~~E~~	

"Give me liberty or give me death!" Patrick Henry

Teaching Notes

What is a Quizzler?

A quotation quizzler is a unique puzzle that combines a puzzle with a quotation. Solving the puzzle requires critical thinking, word analysis, flexible thinking, and the ability to see both the small pieces of the puzzle and the way they fit together to make a whole solution. All the pieces of the puzzle are contained in one compact grid, and when the letters are arranged correctly, they spell out a quote, thus providing exposure to some of the world's greatest thinkers. It's a simple concept that presents both an intellectual challenge and an opportunity to explore the thoughts of famous people.

Classroom Use

These unique puzzles are the perfect venue for honing problem solving skills. As students seek a solution, they use a variety of thinking skills – deductive reasoning, flexible thinking, word analysis, context analysis, grammatical syntax, trial and verification, and sentence composition.

Once students have been introduced to quizzlers and understand how to solve them, there are many uses for these motivating puzzles in the classroom. They can be used for:

- short, sponge activities to fill extra time at the beginning of class or before dismissal
- independent work
- team competitions
- a way to incorporate logical thinking into language arts
- homework assignments
- a preface to studying a famous person, a content area, or a period of history
- an introduction for a lesson with a philosophical or interpersonal focus.

Students find these puzzle both challenging and fun. Because of this built-in motivation, they are the ideal beginnings for other class activities. Once completed, you can dis-cuss who made the quote, what the quotation means, why this person made the quote, why it is significant given the speaker's life or work, and how students can find the quote applicable to their lives. Discussing the speaker and his or her contributions exposes students to a variety of people who have made a difference in their fields, thus providing personal connections to history and role models.

Finding Solutions

Each quotation quizzler uses a famous quote contained in a grid. Each unshaded box on the grid contains one letter from the quote. The shaded boxes indicate spaces between words. At the bottom of each column on the grid is a large box with several letters written vertically. Each of these letters belongs in one of the boxes in the column above it. To solve the puzzle students must use logic, trial and error, and vocabulary knowledge to unscramble the letters in the larger boxes at the bottom and place them in the smaller boxes, thus completing the quote. Punctuation is included in the grid.

A sample quizzler and solution is presented on pages four and five. As you work through a sample quizzler with students for the first time, try first placing letters in columns where there are the fewest letters. Then look for small words. Go back and forth between spaces that have already been filled in and letters that are still unused. Cross out letters as they are used.

Start with the shorter quotations and work up to quizzlers with longer quotes. Once students have worked through a couple of quizzlers on their own, discuss successful strategies they have used. Part of a successful solution is trial and error, but much of it is finding a logical way to analyze each space on the grid and relate it to the surrounding spaces.

1

									,
							.		
H	F	L	W	T	S	M	F	E	R
O	E		A	A	I	A	E	O	T
A	E		W	N	S		N	O	
	L			A			G		

2

							?				,			
									!					
W	N	N	F	F	L	I	M	G	G	S	H	H	T	S
O	H	Y	A	R	E	T	A	L	I	T	O	A	E	
	W		E	N	O	I	T	B	O		T	U	T	
					U									

3

								.		
H	N	N	A	W	H	A	L	N	W	Y
I	U	T	T	I	E		A	O	L	E
R	I			H	E		T	T	N	G
					M		O			

4

					,							.
K	F	L	P	U	A	S	F	L	P	S	Y	R
I	U	E	L	S	T	E	R	O	U	H	E	N
W	E	T	A	H	H	T	M	P	N	A	B	S
B	L	T	T	O	I	O	P	I	T	G	H	
A	I	L	T	T	N	U		A	I	I	O	
B	U								M	M	N	

									,	
								.		
A	N	P	R	R	R	T	N	M	I
I	P	A	A	I	E	I	M	G	Y
		D	D	T	T	M	N	M	Y
		D	I	E	H	E			
				N	N	A			
					A				

						.				
S	M	O	T	T	H	N	N	D	T	F
E	U	S	R	I	O	I	S		H	E
M	H	O	I	C		A				

7

										.
W	**W**	**E**	**M**	**K**	**I**	**F**	**D**	**A**	**E**	**S**
O	**H**	**F**	**R**	**I**	**E**	**A**	**L**	**R**	**Y**	**D**
A	**N**	**I**	**N**	**B**	**E**	**N**	**O**	**O**	**I**	
T	**H**	**O**					**M**		**U**	

8

									,			.
T	**U**	**D**	**H**	**T**	**B**	**C**	**T**	**S**	**R**	**T**	**A**	**T**
A	**O**	**O**	**I**	**E**	**V**	**E**	**E**	**G**	**E**	**E**	**O**	**O**
M	**P**	**S**	**T**	**A**	**N**	**E**		**H**	**R**	**R**	**A**	**T**
	U		**E**		**S**			**G**		**E**	**E**	

9

												.
T	R	E	P	T	N	S	S	B	I	E	I	S
G	H	S	A	O	N	E	I	I	C	L	O	F
R	E	E				P	R	S				Y

10

								;	
									.
S	W	T	H	N	E	E	G	G	O
H	A	H	E	I	C	V	U	O	E
	O	O	E	R	E	A	S	R	
	W	M	T	E	N	R	E	S	
		P	T	H	E	Y	S	R	
		H	P	H	Y	V	E	S	
			E		E				

D	N	M	E	D	H	S	P	G	E
I	O	O	O	M	E	T	A	E	D
S	O	U	E	N	N	I	N	B	
C	D	N	I	R	G	R	N	I	
	O	N	E	T	E	U		T	
	Y	T	U	V	R	O			
		O	E						
		S	L						

12

			.									
T	A	S	F	I	V	G		T	P	R	R	D
H	E	A	G	T	N	T		A	E	D	E	I
W	Y	R	T	E	E	O		U	I	R	M	Y
S	O		T	I	O	E		W	N		E	
M	U											

13

	.									
Y	H	Y	U	T	C	T	N	G	D	T
D	O	E	O	U	U	A	N	I	O	O
T	Y	U		M	H	I	T	N	N	K
	O	O				S	H		S	

14

		,								
										!
D	**T**	**P**	**F**	**S**	**S**	**I**	**B**	**L**	**E**	
O	**O**	**S**	**O**	**H**	**E**	**N**	**D**	**O**		
I	**M**		**T**	**U**	**N**		**T**			
I	**F**			**K**	**I**					

15

										,
										.
B	**O**	**D**	**E**	**R**	**I**	**S**	**T**	**C**	**G**	**M**	**M**
A	**T**	**M**	**T**	**L**	**T**	**H**	**E**	**O**	**E**	**I**	**N**
Y	**E**	**U**	**E**	**S**	**E**	**A**	**A**	**N**	**A**	**L**	
S	**N**	**S**			**O**	**N**	**I**	**N**	**R**	**S**	
	O	**H**			**E**	**M**	**R**	**R**			

16

S	S	F	A	M	B	T	T	N	D
I	E	H	E	A	D	E	A	I	I
R	O	E	E	N	G	E	R	N	D
D	N	M	E	R	N	D	I		I
U	E	D	O	A	R		A		
I				R	S				

17

F	F	V	V	A	C	N	H	H	V	T	T	G
I	F	O	I	N	L	A	E	E	A	R	O	N
L	I	S	H	E	E	R	N	N	K	I	N	P
I	R		E		B	L		A	O	T	I	
			M		I				S	A		
			O									

18

,														
														.
									.					
A	D	E	W	A	D	H	L	L	E	S	D	P	Y	Y
I	N	R	E	D	O	N	I	M	O	P	O	A	H	A
	T	I		A	P	T	E	L	E		E	D		
	V	E			E	V	I	Y	O					
							O	N						

19

												.
K	H	S	D	O	M	G	I	S	H	R	N	E
T	I	E	O	W	N	L	O	Y	O	I	U	G
W	N	O	W	I	N	N	Y	T	T	U	N	
	K	N		O					T	I		

20

									.

N	H	A	M	A	G	S	C	D	N
T	I	T	E	E	N	I	A	A	E
W	T	H	D	I	N	R	S	E	L
	O		T				O	U	
			H				M		

21

												,
												,
												.

C	F	H	C	H	H	P	D	A	W	N	M	L
O	O	E	E	O	O	E	D	D	O	E	S	E
T	T	O	N	T	T	T	F	U	P	E	L	T
D	H	N	T	M	I	N	R	R	E	A	R	T
	I	N		E	N	T	R	E	T	E	N	
	D			N	E				T	U		
	O								S	A		

										—	
											.
P	N	S	S	P	P	I	C	C	Y	S	N
I	I	E	P	I	I	R	R	I	E	T	T
A	N	E	E	P	R	A	A	T	I	O	
N	E	D	N	I	U	N	T	T	I	N	
O	N	R		N	P	E	E	E	O	N	
	G	N			E	R			N		
					I	S					

				,									
						.							
C	E	L	H	E	V	G	Y	Y	T	U	A	N	E
O	A	N	I	D	O	E	A	O	O	H	I	O	G
B	R	W	N	O	T	H	H	R	U		Y	R	U
				R	T	E	E	T					
				E	I								

24

										.
T	H	T	H	C	W	W	T	H	L	D
T	O	U	U	E	H	A	O	G	I	E
Y	Y	E	S	E	U	S	N	R	E	N
	O	O		M	E	I	S		B	

25

									.
C	T	H	E	S	B	S	D	T	M
H	O	A	E	W	I	O	O	I	N
T	O	N	P	F	T	R	S	K	S
	H	E		T	I	R		I	
	H	F			E	Y		O	

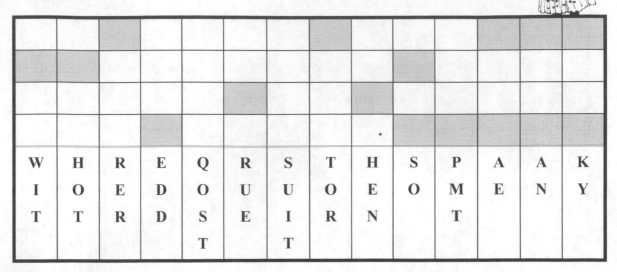

								.					
W	H	R	E	Q	R	S	T	H	S	P	A	A	K
I	O	E	D	O	U	U	O	E	O	M	E	N	Y
T	T	R	D	S	E	I	R	N		T			
	T			T		T							

				;						
								.		
H	H	D	O	E	C	C	N	N	L	T
L	A	R	E	V	E	H	A	U	O	Y
	D	A	T		T	A	O	N	T	
	O	V	I				A	T		
		T	E				O	N		

Puzzle 28 — letter tiles:

B	W	L	U	L	W	O	S	L	T	R
A	O	O	A	B	E	A	A	O	E	I
N	S	T	I	V	E		N	O	D	
	S		A		D		U	T		
	E				M		S			

Puzzle 29 — letter tiles:

L	B	W	E	G	E	T	S	E	W	T	A	N	O
O	I	I	V	E	A	U	N	O	E	H	T	O	
	G	F	I	S		X	I	D	N	R		T	
		L	E			U	P		C				

30

							,				
								.			
T	A	T	N	W	E	D	L	D	P	U	R
M	O	R	A	I	W	I	E	M	U	O	T
P	U	A	K	N	I	N	R	N	D	O	T
W	A	M		A	N	A	N		T	S	
		N			K	L	D				
					N						

31

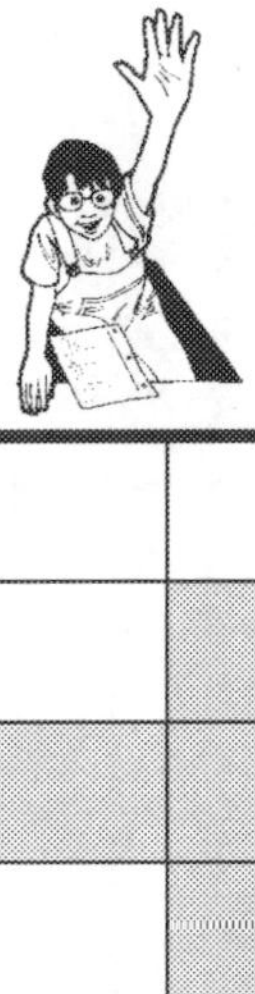

					,							
												.
S	O	T	L	R	O	M	B	B	F	H	R	E
W	U	H	A	I	N	I	H	A	E	I	E	G
P	T	R	L	D	E	T	E	T	T	E	N	
	I	L	E	S		T	N	E	H	O	N	
				Y					T			

32

T	S	C	B	E	D	I	T	N	N	N
I	O	O	R	W	A	K	R	E	E	G
S	N	M	E	E	T	H	I	O	W	
	I	S	M	W	H	I	B	I	G	
	O			E		E	N	L		

33

P	F	V	Y	L	V	E	Y	O	H	G	M
I	E	O	E	O	E	O	J	T	U	E	E
T	O	L	L	O	N			U	I	M	E
H	A		P		U			T	D		

34

The grid has 5 rows (with a comma at the end of row 3 and a period at the end of row 5), above the following lettered columns:

T	F	D	T	H	U	K	G	R	G	D	N
W	H	E	Y	A	A	O	U	E	N	O	E
O	I	E	N	O	Y	R	N	O	O	P	T
A	N			H	E	N			T	E	
T	O										

35

The grid has 6 rows (with a period at the end of row 6), above the following lettered columns:

B	Y	T	O	R	O	G	C	F	O	M
C	E	U	H	I	S	E	E	O	U	O
Y	A	N	U	X	P	V	L	T	T	F
	O	O	E	H	A	E	T	H	E	
		F		R	N		Y			
				D	E		S			

36

R	R	S	E	Q	B	A	R	J	Y	S	T	E
E	E	M	S	U	L	E	A	E	U	H	A	T
L	L	Y	A	O	U	V	T	R	L	O	N	
	I	B	E	L	E	U	E	R	E	Y		
	A	N	I	M	W	E	Y	S	T			
	U	K	O									
			E									

37

Y	V	E	T	L	V	F	J	R	C	T
A	U	G	H	O	U	G	E	A	H	U
R	R	U	L	O	T	E	R	T	O	K
R	I	N	Y	T	I	N	R	T	I	E
E	O	I	N		O	T	E	U	S	F
	S	E				H		Y	E	

T	S	C	C	C	M	M	L	N	W	C	Y
U	H	I	O	O	O	I	O	O	A	A	E
I	N	E	N	T	M	L	N	E	N	A	
			X	G	E	O	D			N	
				M			N				.

M	A	N	S	L	P	O	R	T	B	C	T	R	R
H	I	P	A	E	N	D	U	A	E	A	A	E	E
	O	R	P	I	C	A	N	N	Y	L	N	D	D
						E	S	S		Y	Y	D	
							S	S					.

Puzzle 40 — letter tiles (by column):

U	A	T	D	F	R	C	E	R	V	T	R	B	E	M
I	N	I	A	L	T	H	A	E	E	A	D	G	L	E
		N	N	W		I	H	S	M	E	N	H	I	L
		S	I			T	E			A				
						E								

Puzzle 41 — letter tiles (by column):

L	H	C	C	F	S	M	M	S	B	S	B	D
W	U	I	U	H	E	E	I	O	T	E	O	E
S	O	V	C	E	E	T	R	S	N	A		
	I	L	I	L	D	S	O	O	T	O		
		F	E	N		S	U	S	N			
				D			S					
							I					

Letter bank (columns):

C	O	O	T	V	C	A	R	C	T	H	N	T	D
N	H	N	E	E	E	D	Y	Y	H	U	O	E	G
T	O	A	N	T	C	A	N	D	O	N	N	N	S
C	H	T	T	B	E	R	C	O	B	N	T	T	
T	A	U			V	O	U	N	U	I	I	G	
		A			E	E	N	T	T	S			
										E			

Letter bank (columns):

M	W	C	G	K	S	N	W	R	R	B	Y	F
D	O	U	O	U	P	O	E	E	E	H	E	L
	R	S	R	D	U	S	E	D	T	F	O	
	M	A	N		R	S	D				U	
		O	T		I		A					

44

													’	
														,
								.						
						,								
	,													
										.				
C	I	K	C	C	A	S	T	M	D	I	F	N	G	G
I	F	U	A	H	T	U	O	U	E	T	A	U	R	E
I	H	A	N	Y	E	N	G	T	C	H	D	I	N	T
L	O		E	G	O	N	I	E		E	H	O	N	
Y	T			T	A	I	T			Y	O			

45

						.			
M	T	A	B	E	D	T	H	H	E
I	I	N	K	S	S	Y	T	A	T
	M		I	O		T	H	E	
			D						

													.
S	F	B	C	P	S	S	R	P	U	B	G	D	Y
O	H	E	O	L	H	C	E	R	R	I	E	O	F
T	U	N	S	E	A	E	L	I	U	N	N	G	
	B	C	Y	T	P	O	D	T	M	N	I	S	
	O	E		T	S	T		I	P			T	
						D		E	S				

47

Y	Y	C	U	D	E	C	E	A	S	H	M	L	V	T	G
T	A	U	C	O	M	R	L	I	H	A	T	E	I	E	R
	O	O		G	A	P	L	W	W	E	L	E	N	N	
	O				E	T			R	I					

48

B	A	F	K	R	F	R	D	S	T	D	E	F
C	I	O	E	E	I	A	F	A	Y	G	I	E
H	R	N	N	M	S	S	M	I	R	H	A	T
L	R	E	D	B	T	A	S	L	N	T	I	D
D	O	L	A	O	I		W	T			O	
			D		N		F	O				
					E							

49

M	F	N	F	E	A	W	T	L	T	C	L	S
I	A	A	R	F	R	I	U	E	I	H	O	E
W	N	N	T	H	O	S	P	I	E	I	N	W
O	I		W	I	A	C	O	N	O	B	E	
	H			O	N	K		N		I	E	
					A					S		

50

P	H	V	P	R	O	P	P	C	A	S	V	H	S	O	T
T	E	O	H	A	N	O	I	H	G	I	U	I	I	H	U
H	A	O	U	T	E	L	L	U	E	T	R	T	G	I	N
	Y	E	E	L	P	E	T	N	R	T	C	E	Y	O	T
				O	O	N	Y	T	E	S	U	E			
				C	T	S	S	F	I		S				
					S										

Solutions

1. Ben Johnson

He was not of an age, he was for all time.
See biography on page 52.

H	E		W	A	S		N	O	T
O	F		A	N		A	G	E,	
H	E		W	A	S		F	O	R
A	L	L		T	I	M	E.		

2. Mark Twain

Why not go out on a limb? That's where all the fruit is!
See biography on page 58.

W	H	Y		N	O	T		G	O		O	U	T	
O	N		A		L	I	M	B?		T	H	A	T'	S
	W	H	E	R	E		A	L	L		T	H	E	
			F	R	U	I	T		I	S!				

3. Henry David Thoreau

In the long run we only hit what we aim at.
See biography on page 58.

I	N		T	H	E		L	O	N	G
R	U	N		W	E		O	N	L	Y
H	I	T		W	H	A	T		W	E
			A	I	M		A	T.		

4. Frank Lloyd Wright

If automation keeps up, man will atrophy all his limbs but the push button finger.
See biography on page 60.

I	F		A	U	T	O	M	A	T	I	O	N
K	E	E	P	S		U	P,		M	A	N	
W	I	L	L		A	T	R	O	P	H	Y	
A	L	L		H	I	S		L	I	M	B	S
B	U	T		T	H	E		P	U	S	H	
B	U	T	T	O	N		F	I	N	G	E	R.

5. Vincent van Gogh

I dream my painting, and then I paint my dream.
See biography on page 59.

I			D	R	E	A	M			M	Y
	P	A	I	N	T	I	N	G,		
A	N	D		T	H	E	N			I
		P	A	I	N	T			M	Y
			D	R	E	A	M.			

6. Leo Tolstoy

Music is the shorthand of emotion.
See biography on page 58.

M	U	S	I	C		I	S		T	H	E
S	H	O	R	T	H	A	N	D		O	F
E	M	O	T	I	O	N.					

7. Ralph Waldo Emerson

A friend is one before whom I may think aloud.
See biography on page 51.

A		F	R	I	E	N	D		I	S
O	N	E		B	E	F	O	R	E	
W	H	O	M		I		M	A	Y	
T	H	I	N	K		A	L	O	U	D.

8. Walt Whitman

To have great poets there must be great audiences, too.
See biography on page 59.

T	O		H	A	V	E		G	R	E	A	T
	P	O	E	T	S		T	H	E	R	E	
M	U	S	T		B	E		G	R	E	A	T
A	U	D	I	E	N	C	E	S,		T	O	O.

9. Sir Winston Churchill

The price of greatness is responsibility.
See biography on page 49.

T	H	E				P	R	I	C	E		O	F
G	R	E	A	T	N	E	S	S				I	S
R	E	S	P	O	N	S	I	B	I	L	I	T	Y.

10. Oscar Wilde

Some cause happiness wherever they go; others whenever they go.
See biography on page 60.

S	O	M	E		C	A	U	S	E
H	A	P	P	I	N	E	S	S	
	W	H	E	R	E	V	E	R	
		T	H	E	Y		G	O;	
		O	T	H	E	R	S		
	W	H	E	N	E	V	E	R	
			T	H	E	Y		G	O.

11. Amelia Earhart

Never interrupt someone doing something you said couldn't be done.
See biography on page 50.

		N	E	V	E	R			
I	N	T	E	R	R	U	P	T	
		S	O	M	E	O	N	E	
	D	O	I	N	G				
S	O	M	E	T	H	I	N	G	
	Y	O	U			S	A	I	D
C	O	U	L	D	N'	T		B	E
D	O	N	E.						

12. Rosa Parks

My feet were hurting and I was too tired to give up my seat.
See biography on page 55.

M	Y		F	E	E	T		W	E	R	E	
H	U	R	T	I	N	G		A	N	D		I
W	A	S		T	O	O		T	I	R	E	D
T	O		G	I	V	E		U	P		M	Y
S	E	A	T.									

13. Eleanor Roosevelt

You must do the things you think you cannot do.
See biography on page 56.

Y	O	U		M	U	S	T		D	O
T	H	E		T	H	I	N	G	S	
		Y	O	U		T	H	I	N	K
	Y	O	U		C	A	N	N	O	T
D	O.									

14. Walt Disney

It's kind of fun to do the impossible!
See biography on page 50.

I	T'	S		K	I	N	D		
O	F		F	U	N		T	O	
D	O		T	H	E				
I	M	P	O	S	S	I	B	L	E!

15. Willa Cather

There are some things you learn best in calm, and some in storm.
See biography on page 48.

	T	H	E	R	E		A	R	E		
S	O	M	E		T	H	I	N	G	S	
Y	O	U		L	E	A	R	N			
B	E	S	T		I	N		C	A	L	M,
A	N	D		S	O	M	E			I	N
						S	T	O	R	M.	

16. Confucius

I hear and I forget. I see and I remember. I do and I understand.
See biography on page 49.

I		H	E	A	R		A	N	D
I		F	O	R	G	E	T.		I
S	E	E		A	N	D		I	
R	E	M	E	M	B	E	R.		I
D	O		A	N	D		I		
U	N	D	E	R	S	T	A	N	D.

17. Emily Dickinson

If I can stop one heart from breaking, I shall not live in vain.
See biography on page 49.

I	F		I		C	A	N		S	T	O	P
			O	N	E		H	E	A	R	T	
F	R	O	M		B	R	E	A	K	I	N	G,
I		S	H	A	L	L		N	O	T		
L	I	V	E		I	N			V	A	I	N.

18. Charlie Brown

I've developed a new philosophy. I only dread one day at a time.
See biography on page 48.

I'	V	E		D	E	V	E	L	O	P	E	D		A
	N	E	W		P	H	I	L	O	S	O	P	H	Y.
		I			O	N	L	Y						
	D	R	E	A	D		O	N	E		D	A	Y	
A	T			A		T	I	M	E.					

19. Socrates

The only true wisdom is in knowing you know nothing.
See biography on page 57.

T	H	E		O	N	L	Y		T	R	U	E
W	I	S	D	O	M		I	S		I	N	
K	N	O	W	I	N	G		Y	O	U		
	K	N	O	W		N	O	T	H	I	N	G.

20. Frederick Douglass

The soul that is within me no man can degrade.
See biography on page 50.

		T	H	E			S	O	U	L
T	H	A	T			I	S			
W	I	T	H	I	N		M	E		
N	O		M	A	N		C	A	N	
			D	E	G	R	A	D	E.	

21. Buddha

Do not dwell in the past, do not dream of the future, concentrate the mind on the present.
See biography on page 48.

		D	O		N	O	T		D	W	E	L	L
		I	N		T	H	E			P	A	S	T,
D	O		N	O	T		D	R	E	A	M		
O	F		T	H	E		F	U	T	U	R	E,	
C	O	N	C	E	N	T	R	A	T	E			
T	H	E		M	I	N	D		O	N			
	T	H	E			P	R	E	S	E	N	T.	

22. Thomas Edison

Genius is one percent inspiration and ninety-nine percent perspiration.
See biography on page 50.

	G	E	N	I	U	S			I	S	
O	N	E		P	E	R	C	E	N	T	
I	N	S	P	I	R	A	T	I	O	N	
A	N	D		N	I	N	E	T	Y	-	
N	I	N	E		P	E	R	C	E	N	T
P	E	R	S	P	I	R	A	T	I	O	N.

23. Henry Ford

Whether you believe you can do a thing or not, you are right.
See biography on page 51.

		W	H	E	T	H	E	R			Y	O	U
B	E	L	I	E	V	E		Y	O	U			
C	A	N		D	O		A		T	H	I	N	G
O	R		N	O	T,		Y	O	U		A	R	E
				R	I	G	H	T.					

24. Mohandas Gandhi

You must be the change you wish to see in the world.
See biography on page 52.

Y	O	U		M	U	S	T		B	E
T	H	E		C	H	A	N	G	E	
	Y	O	U		W	I	S	H		
T	O		S	E	E				I	N
	T	H	E		W	O	R	L	D.	

25. Thomas Jefferson

Honesty is the first chapter in the book of wisdom.
See biography on page 52.

H	O	N	E	S	T	Y		I	S
T	H	E		F	I	R	S	T	
C	H	A	P	T	E	R		I	N
	T	H	E		B	O	O	K	
	O	F		W	I	S	D	O	M.

26. Chief Joseph

It does not require many words to speak the truth.
See biography on page 49.

I	T		D	O	E	S		N	O	T			
		R	E	Q	U	I	R	E		M	A	N	Y
W	O	R	D	S		T	O		S	P	E	A	K
T	H	E		T	R	U	T	H.					

27. Martin Luther King, Jr.

Hate cannot drive out hate; only love can do that.
See biography on page 53.

H	A	T	E		C	A	N	N	O	T
	D	R	I	V	E		O	U	T	
	H	A	T	E;			O	N	L	Y
L	O	V	E			C	A	N		
		D	O		T	H	A	T.		

39

28. Abraham Lincoln

As I would not be a slave, so I would not be a master.
See biography on page 54.

A	S		I		W	O	U	L	D	
N	O	T		B	E		A			
	S	L	A	V	E,		S	O		I
	W	O	U	L	D		N	O	T	
B	E		A		M	A	S	T	E	R.

29. Margaret Mitchell

Life's under no obligation to give us what we expect.
See biography on page 55.

L	I	F	E'	S		U	N	D	E	R		N	O
O	B	L	I	G	A	T	I	O	N		T	O	
	G	I	V	E		U	S		W	H	A	T	
		W	E		E	X	P	E	C	T.			

30. John F. Kennedy

Mankind must put an end to war, or war will put an end to mankind.
See biography on page 53.

M	A	N	K	I	N	D		M	U	S	T
P	U	T		A	N		E	N	D		
T	O			W	A	R,			O	R	
W	A	R		W	I	L	L		P	U	T
		A	N		E	N	D		T	O	
		M	A	N	K	I	N	D.			

31. Shel Silverstein

Put something silly in the world that ain't been there before.
See biography on page 57.

P	U	T		S	O	M	E	T	H	I	N	G
S	I	L	L	Y		I	N		T	H	E	
W	O	R	L	D		T	H	A	T			
			A	I	N'	T		B	E	E	N	
	T	H	E	R	E		B	E	F	O	R	E.

32. Carl Sagan

Somewhere, something incredible is waiting to be known.
See biography on page 47.

S	O	M	E	W	H	E	R	E,			
	S	O	M	E	T	H	I	N	G		
I	N	C	R	E	D	I	B	L	E		
	I	S		W	A	I	T	I	N	G	
T	O		B	E		K	N	O	W	N.	

33. Mother Theresa

If you judge people you have no time to love them.
See biography on page 55.

I	F		Y	O	U		J	U	D	G	E
P	E	O	P	L	E		Y	O	U		
H	A	V	E		N	O		T	I	M	E
T	O		L	O	V	E		T	H	E	M.

34. Franklin D. Roosevelt

When you get to the end of your rope, tie a knot and hang on.
See biography on page 56.

W	H	E	N		Y	O	U		G	E	T
T	O		T	H	E		E	N	D		
O	F		Y	O	U	R		R	O	P	E,
T	I	E		A		K	N	O	T		
A	N	D		H	A	N	G			O	N.

35. Michael Jordan

You have to expect things of yourself before you can do them.
See biography on page 53.

Y	O	U		H	A	V	E		T	O
			E	X	P	E	C	T		
		T	H	I	N	G	S		O	F
	Y	O	U	R	S	E	L	F		
B	E	F	O	R	E		Y	O	U	
C	A	N		D	O		T	H	E	M.

41

36. Margaret Mead

Always remember that you are absolutely unique. Just like everyone else.
See biography on page 54.

			A	L	W	A	Y	S				
R	E	M	E	M	B	E	R		T	H	A	T
		Y	O	U			A	R	E			
	A	B	S	O	L	U	T	E	L	Y		
	U	N	I	Q	U	E.		J	U	S	T	
L	I	K	E		E	V	E	R	Y	O	N	E
E	L	S	E.									

37. Will Rogers

Even if you are on the right track, you'll get run over if you just sit there.
See biography on page 56.

E	V	E	N		I	F		Y	O	U
A	R	E			O	N		T	H	E
R	I	G	H	T		T	R	A	C	K,
Y	O	U'	L	L		G	E	T		
R	U	N		O	V	E	R		I	F
			Y	O	U		J	U	S	T
	S	I	T		T	H	E	R	E.	

38. Booker T. Washington

Excellence is to do a common thing in an uncommon way.
See biography on page 59.

		E	X	C	E	L	L	E	N	C	E
I	S			T	O		D	O		A	
			C	O	M	M	O	N			
T	H	I	N	G		I	N		A	N	
U	N	C	O	M	M	O	N		W	A	Y.

39. George Washington

Happiness and moral duty are inseparably connected.
See biography on page 59.

H	A	P	P	I	N	E	S	S		A	N	D	
M	O	R	A	L		D	U	T	Y		A	R	E
	I	N	S	E	P	A	R	A	B	L	Y		
					C	O	N	N	E	C	T	E	D.

40. Michelangelo

I saw the angel in the marble and carved until I set him free.
See biography on page 54.

I		S	A	W		T	H	E		A	N	G	E	L
		I	N		T	H	E		M	A	R	B	L	E
	A	N	D			C	A	R	V	E	D			
U	N	T	I	L		I		S	E	T		H	I	M
				F	R	E	E.							

41. Helen Keller

Life is a succession of lessons which must be lived to be understood.
See biography on page 53.

		L	I	F	E		I	S		A			
S	U	C	C	E	S	S	I	O	N				
	O	F		L	E	S	S	O	N	S			
W	H	I	C	H		M	U	S	T		B	E	
L	I	V	E	D		T	O		B	E			
			U	N	D	E	R	S	T	O	O	D.	

42. Albert Einstein

Not everything that can be counted counts, and not everything that counts can be counted.
See biography on page 51.

N	O	T		E	V	E	R	Y	T	H	I	N	G
T	H	A	T		C	A	N		B	E			
C	O	U	N	T	E	D		C	O	U	N	T	S,
						A	N	D		N	O	T	
			E	V	E	R	Y	T	H	I	N	G	
T	H	A	T		C	O	U	N	T	S			
C	A	N		B	E		C	O	U	N	T	E	D.

43. Rudyard Kipling

Words are, of course, the most powerful drug used by mankind.
See biography on page 54.

	W	O	R	D	S		A	R	E,		O	F
		C	O	U	R	S	E,		T	H	E	
M	O	S	T		P	O	W	E	R	F	U	L
D	R	U	G		U	S	E	D		B	Y	
	M	A	N	K	I	N	D.					

44. Maya Angelou

If you don't like something, change it. If you can't change it, change your attitude.
See biography on page 48.

I	F		Y	O	U						D	O	N'	T
L	I	K	E			S	O	M	E	T	H	I	N	G,
C	H	A	N	G	E		I	T.		I	F			
Y	O	U		C	A	N'	T		C	H	A	N	G	E
I	T,		C	H	A	N	G	E		Y	O	U	R	
		A	T	T	I	T	U	D	E.					

45. Sojourner Truth

It is the mind that makes the body.
See biography on page 58.

I	T		I	S			T	H	E
M	I	N	D			T	H	A	T
	M	A	K	E	S		T	H	E
			B	O	D	Y.			

46. Ayn Rand

The ladder of success is best climbed by stepping on the rungs of opportunity.
See biography on page 56.

T	H	E		L	A	D	D	E	R			O	F
S	U	C	C	E	S	S		I	S				
	B	E	S	T		C	L	I	M	B	E	D	
		B	Y		S	T	E	P	P	I	N	G	
	O	N		T	H	E		R	U	N	G	S	
O	F		O	P	P	O	R	T	U	N	I	T	Y.

47. Georgia O'Keeffe

You get whatever accomplishment you are willing to declare.
See biography on page 55.

Y	O	U		G	E	T		W	H	A	T	E	V	E	R
	A	C	C	O	M	P	L	I	S	H	M	E	N	T	
	Y	O	U		A	R	E		W	I	L	L	I	N	G
T	O			D	E	C	L	A	R	E.					

48. Langston Hughes

Hold fast to dreams, for if dreams die, life is a broken winged bird that cannot fly.
See biography on page 52.

H	O	L	D		F	A	S	T		T	O	
D	R	E	A	M	S,		F	O	R		I	F
			D	R	E	A	M	S		D	I	E,
L	I	F	E		I	S		A				
B	R	O	K	E	N		W	I	N	G	E	D
				B	I	R	D		T	H	A	T
C	A	N	N	O	T		F	L	Y.			

49. William Shakespeare

What a piece of work is man! How noble in reason! How infinite in faculties!
See biography on page 57.

W	H	A	T		A		P	I	E	C	E	
O	F		W	O	R	K			I	S		
M	A	N!		H	O	W		N	O	B	L	E
I	N		R	E	A	S	O	N!		H	O	W
	I	N	F	I	N	I	T	E		I	N	
				F	A	C	U	L	T	I	E	S!

50. Benjamin Franklin

The constitution only gives people the right to pursue happiness. You have to catch it yourself.
See biography on page 51.

T	H	E		C	O	N	S	T	I	T	U	T	I	O	N
				O	N	L	Y		G	I	V	E	S		
P	E	O	P	L	E		T	H	E		R	I	G	H	T
			T	O		P	U	R	S	U	E				
		H	A	P	P	I	N	E	S	S.		Y	O	U	
H	A	V	E		T	O		C	A	T	C	H		I	T
	Y	O	U	R	S	E	L	F.							

46

Who Said It?

An Alphabetical Listing of People Quoted

Person   **Quizzler number**

Biographical Information

Brief Biographies of People Quoted

Maya Angelou

Maya Angelou (1928 -) is an American author and poet whose most popular writings are autobiographical in nature. The first book in her series of memoirs, *I Know Why the Caged Bird Sings*, emphasizes themes of courage, determination, and the achievement of one's highest potential. Her writings frequently include portrayals of strong African American women. Angelou composed the poem "On the Pulse of Morning," which she recited at the inauguration of President Bill Clinton in January 1993.

Charlie Brown

Charlie Brown is the well-known creation of Charles Schulz (1922-2000), American artist and cartoonist. Schulz's comic strip "Peanuts" debuted on October 2, 1950 and is one of the most popular strips in history, appearing in more than 2,000 newspapers and translated into more than two dozen languages. Award-winning animated television specials and hundreds of "Peanuts" books and other products continue to be vastly popular, though Schulz died in 2000. Charlie Brown and his dog, Snoopy, are the most well-known of the Peanuts characters.

Buddha

Buddha (563? - 483? BC) was a philosopher and teacher born in Nepal. His philosophical teachings became the foundation of Buddhism, a religion that has influenced the lives of millions of people for nearly 2,500 years. Buddha was considered a man of integrity, compassion and deep thought. The name Buddha means "Enlightened One."

Willa Cather

Willa Cather (1873-1947) is considered to be one of America's leading novelists. Her skillful writing portrays clear pictures of the American landscape and the people it influenced. Much of Catcher's writing is set in Nebraska and the American Southwest and typically focuses on the contrast between infringement of cities upon the wilderness and the accomplishments of the people who settled there. Her sturdy, determined female characters commonly face difficulty relating to a society where women are expected to be dependent.

Chief Joseph

Chief Joseph (1840? -1904) was a chief of the Nez Percé Native Americans who led his people in a resistance against white invasion. His Nez Percé name was In-mut-too-yah-lat-lat, meaning "thunder coming up from the water over the land." In 1877 combat broke out as a result of the United States government's attempts to enforce a treaty that confined the Nez Percé to a reservation. Both sides experienced victories and defeats, but Joseph and his people eventually surrendered and were sent to Oklahoma, where many died. In 1903 Joseph was received in Washington, D.C. by President Theodore Roosevelt.

Sir Winston Churchill

Sir Winston Churchill (1874-1965) was a British politician and the prime minister of the United Kingdom from 1940 to 1945 and 1951 to 1955. He is generally regarded as the greatest British leader of the 20th century. Churchill is famous for his adept leadership during World War II. His strength, determination, political expertise, and tremendous energy allowed him to lead his country through the war, which was considered to be one of the gravest struggles in British history.

Confucius

Confucius (551? - 479? BC) was a Chinese philosopher and is known to be one of the most influential figures in Chinese history. He considered his teachings practical and ethical, rather than religious, and felt it his obligation to reinstate ancient morality. His concept of human duty taught that all acts should be based on the five virtues of kindness, uprightness, decorum, wisdom and faithfulness. His teachings exerted a powerful influence on the Chinese nation for many centuries following his death.

Emily Dickinson

Emily Dickinson (1830-1886) is one of the best-known poets and foremost authors in American literature. Her simple yet emotional writings are considered intensely intellectual and explore a variety of important subjects, including the suffering and rapture of love, the incomprehensible nature of death, the horrors of war, religion, humor, and the significance of literature, music, and art. It is widely believed that few of Dickinson's poems were formally published during her lifetime. She did, however, include a large portion of her poems in the letters she sent regularly to friends and correspondents.

𝒲alt Disney

Walt Disney (1901-1966) was an American cartoon artist and animated film producer. His production company was one of the major producers of films for theaters and television in the 1950s and 1960s and was also involved in the publication of books and the syndication of comic strips. Walt Disney's most popular creations, however, are his famous characters – Mickey Mouse, Goofy, Donald Duck, Pluto, and others – known the world over. In 1955 Disney opened the Disneyland theme park in California. Following his death in 1966 additional parks have opened in Florida, Japan, and France. Disney received 26 Academy Awards for film making during his career.

𝐹rederick Douglass

Frederick Douglass (1817-1895) was an American abolitionist, speaker and writer. He was the son of a slave and was essentially self-educated. An attempt to escape slavery in 1836 failed. Two years later he succeeded and escaped to Massachusetts. Before and during the Civil War, Douglass urged other slaves to escape as well. At an anti-slavery convention in Massachusetts in 1841 he gave an impromptu speech, which was met with great accolades. His work for the Underground Railroad did much to further the cause of the abolitionists. He became a symbol of freedom and achievement among both whites and blacks.

𝒜melia Earhart

Amelia Earhart (1898-1937) was America's most famous female aviator. She was noted for her flights across the Atlantic and Pacific Oceans and her attempt to fly around the world. She became the first woman to fly alone across the Atlantic Ocean in 1932, and in 1935 she was the first woman to fly the Pacific Ocean. In June 1937 she and her navigator began a flight around the world, but their plane disappeared on July 2. Though the United States Navy conducted a thorough search, it failed to discover any trace of the lost flyers. Their fate remains a mystery.

𝒯homas Edison

Thomas Edison (1847-1931) was an American inventor whose research and many technological advances shaped and changed modern society dramatically. He developed, among other things, a practical electric light bulb, an electric generating system, a sound-recording device, and the motion picture projector. All of this, and yet he only attended public school three months in his life! Altogether, Edison patented more than one thousand inventions.

Albert Einstein

Albert Einstein (1879-1955) was the most well-known scientist of the 20th century. A German-born American physicist and Nobel laureate, he is best known for his creation of the theory of relativity and theories concerning light particles. Although he didn't talk until he was three, he was able to understand difficult mathematical concepts at a very early age and taught himself Euclidean geometry when he was only 12 years old. As an adult, Einstein dedicated much of his time and resources to political and social causes, but science always came first. He believed that only the discovery of the nature of the universe would have any lasting meaning.

Ralph Waldo Emerson

Ralph Waldo Emerson (1803-1882) was an American essayist and poet and one of the leaders of the philosophical movement known as Transcendentalism. Emerson's writing is known for its poetic language and its elegant presentation of ideas. He was dedicated to the idea of freedom of the individual and liberation from artificial restraints. *Essays*, *Nature*, and *Self-Reliance* are among Emerson's most popular works.

Henry Ford

Henry Ford (1863-1947) was the well-known American industrialist whose most daring and lasting accomplishments were his achievements in the automobile industry. He became a machinist's apprentice in Detroit, Michigan at the age of 16 and in 1896 built his first automobile. In 1913 he began using assembly-line techniques in his manufacturing plant. Although he did not originate the use of the assembly line, he is credited with making its use common practice. Ford was a great inspiration in the growth of mass production and the raising of the standard of living in the United States.

Benjamin Franklin

Benjamin Franklin (1706-1790) was an American printer, author, diplomat, philosopher, musician, economist, and scientist who contributed greatly to the cause of the American Revolution and to the newly formed government that followed. Because of his notable service to his country, Benjamin Franklin consistently ranks as one of America's greatest citizens. Known for his common sense, wisdom and wit, Franklin is also remembered as being a sharp conversationalist and a considerate listener.

Mohandas Gandhi

Mohandas Gandhi (1869-1948) was an Indian leader, who established his country's freedom through a nonviolent revolution. Gandhi was born in India, but educated in London. He returned to India and attempted unsuccessfully to establish a law practice there. Though Indian by birth, he was treated as an inferior and was quickly dismayed at the widespread denial of civil and political rights of the Indian people. He established a practice known as passive resistance and was imprisoned many times. He cites Leo Tolstoy and Henry David Thoreau as his primary inspirations.

Langston Hughes

Langston Hughes (1902-1967) was an African American writer. After spending time living in Paris, he returned to the United States and worked as a busboy in a Washington, D.C. restaurant. In 1925, he accidentally left three of his poems beside the plate of a famous poet dining in the restaurant. The poet recognized Hughes's literary skills and helped him get published. Hughes is best known for his poetry, which integrates the use of black folk rhythms. In the late 1920s he lived in New York City and was a prominent figure of the Harlem Renaissance.

Thomas Jefferson

Thomas Jefferson (1743-1826) was the third president of the United States and the author of the Declaration of Independence. He is widely regarded as one of the most brilliant individuals in history. He had endless interests, and his many accomplishments were great and varied. Jefferson was a philosopher, educator, naturalist, politician, scientist, architect, inventor, farmer, musician, and writer. He had a deep faith in the right of popular rule, and he aimed to develop a government that would assure freedom for the individual.

Ben Johnson

Ben Johnson (1572-1637) was an English dramatist, poet, actor, and friend of the famous William Shakespeare. (Shakespeare even acted in one of Johnson's plays.) This quote appeared in the dedication to "The First Folio," the first collection of Shakespeare's work to be printed. Ben Johnson wrote this now-famous line following Shakespeare's death in 1626 to commemorate him, predicting that Shakespeare's work would live through the ages. As William Shakespeare is widely considered to be the greatest writer in the history of the English language, it appears that Johnson was right.

Michael Jordan

Michael Jordan (1963-) is a professional American basketball player, generally considered to be the greatest player in the history of basketball. Jordan stands 6' 6" tall and first became popular as a dynamic individual scorer. Jordan led the Chicago Bulls to six National Basketball Association championships (1991-1993, 1996-1998). He was so popular with his fans that many credit him with helping to make basketball one of the world's most popular spectator sports.

Helen Keller

Helen Keller (1880-1968) overcame significant physical handicaps to become a popular and inspirational American author and lecturer. At 19 months old, Helen became sick with a serious illness that left her deaf and blind. She did not begin her education until she was seven years old but quickly learned to read by the Braille system and to write by means of a specially constructed typewriter. At age ten, Keller learned to speak after only one month of study. Helen worked and raised funds during her life for the American Foundation for the Blind. She traveled and spoke in many countries, including Australia, Egypt, England, France, Italy, Japan, and South Africa.

John F. Kennedy

John F. Kennedy (1917-1963) was the 35th president of the United States and the youngest man ever elected to the office. He was also the first Roman Catholic president and the first president to be born in the 20th century. He served as president from 1961 to 1963. He was widely admired by young Americans and is often considered one of America's most popular presidents. His foreign and domestic achievements were noteworthy, though he only served three years of his term as president. Kennedy was assassinated in Dallas, Texas, in 1963.

Martin Luther King, Jr.

Martin Luther King, Jr. (1929-1968) was an American clergyman and Nobel Prize winner. He is considered one of the principal leaders of the civil rights movement during the 1960s in America. King advocated a policy of nonviolent protest, which he modeled after the teachings of Mohandas Gandhi. King peacefully challenged American ideas of segregation and racial discrimination in the 1950s and 1960s and helped convince many white Americans to become more supportive of civil rights in the United States. In 1968 King was assassinated and immediately became a symbol of protest in the struggle for racial justice.

Rudyard Kipling

Rudyard Kipling (1865-1936) was an English writer who authored novels, poems and short stories, set mostly in India and Burma during the time of British rule. He traveled extensively in Asia and the United States and lived briefly in Vermont. He was a prolific writer, and his work was widely popular. He was the first English author to be honored with the Nobel Prize in literature. His most famous works include *The Jungle Book* and *Just So Stories for Little Children*.

Abraham Lincoln

Abraham Lincoln (1809-1865) was the 16th president of the United States and is generally considered to be one of the greatest leaders in American history. His greatest challenge was the preservation of the Union during the Civil War. He believed in the principles of democracy and was always an expert politician, persuading people using his reasoned words and thoughtful deeds. In 1863 he issued the Emancipation Proclamation, which ordered the freeing of all slaves in rebel territory. Lincoln was assassinated in 1865 while watching a performance of "Our American Cousin" at Ford's Theater in Washington, D.C.

Margaret Mead

Margaret Mead (1901-1978) was an American anthropologist, widely respected for her studies of primitive societies and the contributions she made to the field of social anthropology. Mead participated in many field expeditions and conducted celebrated research in Bali, New Guinea and Samoa Islands. Her work focused on the study of cultural child-rearing patterns. Mead investigated contemporary American social problems, particularly those affecting youth, and served on various government committees. She was often a controversial speaker on modern social issues.

Michelangelo

Michelangelo (1475-1564) is without question one of the most inspired masters in the history of art and one of the most powerful forces in the Italian Renaissance. As a sculptor, architect, painter and poet, he exerted an unmistakable influence on his contemporaries and on subsequent Western art in general. His sculptural work integrates formal classical beauty with expressiveness and feeling. Michelangelo is probably most famous for his frescoes on the ceiling of the Sistine Chapel, painted between 1508 and 1512.

Margaret Mitchell

Margaret Mitchell (1900-1949) was an American author, famous for writing one of the most popular novels of all time, *Gone with the Wind*. Her professional life began as a reporter for the *Atlanta Journal*. Mitchell started writing *Gone with the Wind* in 1926 and it took her ten years to complete. Immediate success met this romantic illustration of life in the South during the Civil War, and it was awarded the Pulitzer Prize in 1937. Scarlett O'Hara, the novel's gritty and headstrong protagonist, is one of American literature's most instantly recognized characters. A motion picture of the novel was released in 1939 and quickly became – and remains – one of the most popular films of all time.

Mother Teresa

Mother Teresa (1910-1997) was a Roman Catholic nun and founder of the Missionaries of Charity. In 1948 she was granted permission to leave her post at the convent and begin a ministry among the sick in Calcutta. Mother Teresa opened the Pure Heart Home for Dying Destitutes in Calcutta in 1952 but extended her work to many other parts of the world as well. She is universally recognized as a symbol of compassion, grace and charity. Mother Teresa was awarded the Nobel Peace Prize in 1979 in recognition of her humanitarian efforts.

Georgia O'Keeffe

Georgia O'Keeffe (1887-1986) was an American abstract painter, best known for her large paintings of desert flowers, sun-dried animal skulls, and landscapes of New Mexico, which she fell in love with on her first visit there in 1929. Her paintings typically present single flowers or objects in extreme close-up views, with most of the details so enlarged that they become unfamiliar and surprising. In later years O'Keeffe began integrating aerial themes of clouds and sky into her paintings.

Rosa Parks

Rosa Parks (1913-) is a civil rights pioneer, born in Tuskegee, Alabama. In 1955 she was arrested for violating segregation laws by refusing to give up her seat on a bus to a white passenger. This renowned incident led to a boycott of the bus system by African Americans. The boycott continued, despite much harassment, and in 1956 segregated seating was ruled unconstitutional. Parks later worked as a fund-raiser for the NAACP and was hired to manage the Detroit office of Congressman John Conyers, Jr. She co-founded the Institute for Self Development to help young people reach their full potential and has won numerous awards for her work for civil rights.

Ayn Rand

Ayn Rand (1905-1982) was a Russian-born American novelist and philosopher. She was a controversial figure in twentieth century literature who advocated individualism over collectivism. Rand's essential beliefs, that humans should live for themselves without sacrificing any part of their natures or ideals to other people, permeated her writing. Her two most famous works, *The Fountainhead* and *Atlas Shrugged*, are colossal American classics. In later years, Rand stopped writing fiction and worked as a public speaker.

Will Rogers

Will Rogers (1879-1935) was an American humorist, actor, and writer, born in Indian Territory in what is now Oklahoma. He made a name for himself by premiering a rope-throwing act in a New York City vaudeville house in 1905. He soon became more popular for his humorous monologues than for his rope tricks and eventually began acting in motion pictures and writing newspaper articles. He loved to poke fun at the politicians and celebrities of his day and was noted for his unique, warm, folksy perspective on life. Rogers was killed in an airplane crash in Alaska.

Eleanor Roosevelt

Eleanor Roosevelt (1884-1962), niece of President Theodore Roosevelt, was a social activist, author, lecturer, and first lady. In 1905 she married her distant cousin, Franklin D. Roosevelt who, in 1932, became president of the United States. Though she never officially held an office in her husband's administration, her influence was keenly felt. She was considered more liberal than her husband, and she worked to promote racial equality. She was the U.S. delegate to the United Nations from 1945 to 1953, chairing the commission that drafted the Universal Declaration of Human Rights.

Franklin D. Roosevelt

Franklin D. Roosevelt (1882-1945) was the 32nd president of the United States, serving from 1933 to 1945. He was elected to four terms in office – the most of any president. Roosevelt has the distinction of holding office during two of the greatest crises ever faced by the United States: the Great Depression and World War II. His reform program, known as the New Deal, provided changes in the system of free enterprise and prepared the way for what is now called welfare. Roosevelt had a tremendous impact on the office of president, during both war and peacetime.

Carl Sagan

Carl Sagan (1934-1996) was an American astronomer, author, and professor who worked to make science more popular among and accessible to the general public. He did this through lectures, television appearances and popular books. Though his research spanned many areas of astronomy and cosmology, he was particularly interested in the origin of life on the earth and in the possibility of life elsewhere in the universe. He was a consultant to NASA beginning in the 1950s and was an experimenter on several space expeditions. In addition to authoring a best-selling science book, *Cosmos*, he produced an award-winning television series.

William Shakespeare

William Shakespeare (1564-1616) was an English playwright and poet and is revered by many as the greatest dramatist in the world. His plays communicate a deep and thorough knowledge of human behavior, which he reveals through portrayals of a wide variety of characters. His use of poetry within his plays to express deep levels of human motivation in individual, social, and universal situations is considered one of the greatest accomplishments in literary history. He is credited with writing 37 plays, two narrative poems and 154 sonnets.

Shel Silverstein

Shel Silverstein (1932-1999) was an American writer, cartoonist, illustrator, and musician, but he was best known for his children's poetry. He served with the United States armed forces in Japan and Korea during the 1950s and began drawing cartoons for the military newspaper. He was a cartoonist for adult magazines and a successful composer of folk music. His work was always a mix of serious and silly. He published his first book for children in 1963, which he both wrote and illustrated. *The Giving Tree* and *Where the Sidewalk Ends* are considered his most popular books.

Socrates

Socrates (470? - 399? BC) was a Greek philosopher, whose work made a deep and lasting impact on Western philosophy. Following a typical education in literature, music, and gymnastics, he engaged in a self-directed study of philosophy. Socrates believed firmly in the predominance of debate over writing and spent most of his adult life in the public places of Athens, engaging in dialogue and argument with anyone who would listen. He had a great love of life, was committed to truth, and was socially popular because of his keen wit and a sharp sense of humor.

Henry David Thoreau

Henry David Thoreau (1817-1862) was an American writer, philosopher and naturalist, whose work demonstrates a belief in the importance of individualism. Thoreau devoted most of his time to the study of nature, to meditating on philosophical problems, to reading Greek, Latin, French, and English literature, and to long conversations with neighbors. Only two of his works were actually published during his lifetime. Other books and collections were edited by friends from his journals, manuscripts and letters after his death.

Leo Tolstoy

Leo Tolstoy (1828-1910) was a Russian writer and philosopher, who is generally considered one of the greatest novelists in the world. His writings profoundly influenced much of 20th-century literature, and his moral teachings helped shape the thinking of several important spiritual and political leaders. It was Tolstoy's idea of passive resistance that Mohandas Gandhi applied to India's struggles against British rule. In turn, Gandhi's ideas helped inspire Martin Luther King, Jr. in his efforts for racial justice in the United States. Tolstoy vehemently defended individual personality and conscience. His most famous works are *War and Peace* and *Anna Karenina*.

Sojourner Truth

Sojourner Truth (circa 1797-1883) was an American abolitionist and advocate of women's rights. Born into slavery, she was freed in 1828 when New York emancipated slaves. She began preaching in the streets of New York City when she arrived there in 1829. Truth began touring the country speaking on behalf of the abolitionists and in 1850, after encountering the women's rights movement, she added that to her cause. Abraham Lincoln received her in the White House in 1864. She was an effective, charismatic speaker though she was illiterate all her life.

Mark Twain

Mark Twain (1835-1910) was born with the name Samuel Clemens and is one of America's best-loved authors and humorists. Twain had little formal training in writing. He received most of his education from the print shops and newspaper offices he worked at when he was young. His writing is renowned for its use of social satire and its memorable characters. Mark Twain found inspiration in the untamed West and used it as the setting for much of his writing. Many consider *The Adventures of Huckleberry Finn* to be his masterpiece.

Vincent van Gogh

Vincent van Gogh (1853-1890) was a Dutch painter whose work represents expressionism and emotional inspiration. In his early life he had a variety of careers, including salesman in an art gallery, a French tutor, a theological student, and an evangelist among the miners in Belgium. He was influenced by the work of the impressionists, Pissarro and Seurat, and by the work of Japanese print makers. His paintings are known for their intense, brilliant hues, swirling brush strokes and their distinctive style.

Booker T. Washington

Booker T. Washington (1856-1915) was an American educator, born the son of a slave. Washington began teaching after graduation from Hampton Normal and Agricultural Institute. In 1881 he was appointed principal of a black normal school in Tuskegee, Alabama, now Tuskegee University. Under Washington's leadership, the institution became a major center for industry and agriculture. Washington urged African Americans to improve their status through vocational training and economic self-reliance. More militant blacks, such as writer W. E. B. Du Bois, objected to such accommodating strategies and strongly opposed Washington.

George Washington

George Washington (1732-1799) was the first president of the United States and one of the most important statesmen in U.S. history. His leadership in unifying the American colonies and helping them gain independence is immeasurable. Washington formed the Continental Army from little more than an angry mob and fought and eventually won the Revolutionary War. His direction brought defeat to the British and forced them to grant independence to their most valuable overseas territory. Washington was reluctant to accept the presidency. He did so only as an unselfish act of service to the newly born republic he'd fought so hard to establish.

Walt Whitman

Walt Whitman (1819-1892) was an American poet, whose work powerfully expresses a belief in the worth of the individual and the oneness of all humanity. He broke with the traditions of poetry, and his style left a profound effect on American thought and literature. Whitman issued the first of many editions of *Leaves of Grass* in 1855, and it is still widely popular today. His poetry has been translated into every major language and is widely recognized as having had a deep influence on the work of many American writers such as Hart Crane, William Carlos Williams and Allen Ginsberg.

*O*scar Wilde

Oscar Wilde (1854-1900) was an Irish-born writer and humorist who believed in the principle of art for the sake of art. He was a novelist, playwright, poet and critic. His only novel, *The Picture of Dorian Gray*, is a spectacular tale of moral decline, known for its sharp, precise style. Additionally, Wilde wrote a number of engaging plays, among them *An Ideal Husband, The Importance of Being Earnest*, and *Salomé*, a serious drama about obsessive passion. In 1895, Wilde spent two years doing hard labor in a British prison, having been convicted on a charge of immorality.

*F*rank Lloyd Wright

Frank Lloyd Wright (1867-1959) is considered one of the most influential designers in modern Western architecture. His building designs were innovative and inventive, and he employed a style based on natural forms, which he called "organic architecture." Wright left a unique heritage of existing buildings and designs, and his work continues to influence and inspire architects today.

Listing of Quotations
Alphabetical

Mankind must put an end to war, or war will put an end to mankind.
John F. Kennedy 30

Music is the shorthand of emotion.
Leo Tolsoy 6

My feet were hurting and I was too tired to give up my seat.
Rosa Parks 12

Never interrupt someone doing something you said couldn't be done.
Amelia Earhart 11

Not everything that can be counted counts, and not everything that counts can be counted.
Albert Einstein 42

Put something silly in the world that ain't been there before.
Shel Silverstein 31

Some cause happiness wherever they go; others whenever they go.
Oscar Wilde 10

Somewhere, something incredible is waiting to be known.
Carl Sagan 32

The Constitution only gives people the right to pursue happiness. You have to catch it yourself.
Benjamin Franklin 50

The ladder of success is best climbed by stepping on the rungs of opportunity.
Ayn Rand 46

The only true wisdom is in knowing you know nothing.
Socrates 19

The price of greatness is responsibility.
Sir Winston Churchill 9

The soul that is within me no man can degrade.
Frederick Douglas 20

There are some things you learn best in calm, and some in storm.
Willa Cather 15

To have great poets there must be great audiences, too.
Walt Whitman 8

What a piece of work is man! How noble in reason! How infinite in faculties!
William Shakespeare 49

When you get to the end of your rope, tie a knot and hang on.
Franklin D. Roosevelt 34

Whether you believe you can do a thing or not, you are right.
Henry Ford 23

Why not go out on a limb? That's where all the fruit is!
Mark Twain 2

Words are, of course, the most powerful drug used by mankind.
Rudyard Kipling 43

You get whatever accomplishment you are willing to declare.
Georgia O'Keeffe 47

You have to expect things of yourself before you can do them.
Michael Jordan 35

You must be the change you wish to see in the world.
Mohandas Gandhi 24

You must do the things you think you cannot do.
Eleanor Roosevelt 13

Listing of Quotations

By Themes

Accomplishment

♦ *Even if you are on the right track, you'll get run over if you just sit there.* Will Rogers

♦ *Excellence is to do a common thing in an uncommon way.*
Booker T. Washington

♦ *Genius is one percent inspiration and ninety-nine percent perspiration.*
Thomas Edison

♦ *I saw the angel in the marble and carved until I set him free.* Michelangelo

♦ *Never interrupt someone doing something you said couldn't be done.* Amelia Earhart

♦ *You get whatever accomplishment you are willing to declare.* Georgia O'Keeffe

Arts & Literature

♦ *I dream my painting, and then I paint my dream.* Vincent van Gogh

♦ *If automation keeps up, man will atrophy all his limbs but the push button finger.*
Frank Lloyd Wright

♦ *If I can stop one heart from breaking, I shall not live in vain.* Emily Dickinson

♦ *Music is the shorthand of emotion.*
Leo Tolsoy

♦ *To have great poets there must be great audiences, too.* Walt Whitman

♦ *What a piece of work is man! How noble in reason! How infinite in faculties!*
William Shakespeare

Courage

♦ *Hold fast to dreams, for if dreams die, life is a broken winged bird that cannot fly.*
Langston Hughes

♦ *Life's under no obligation to give us what we expect.* Margaret Mitchell

♦ *Mankind must put an end to war, or war will put an end to mankind.* John F. Kennedy

♦ *My feet were hurting and I was too tired to give up my seat.* Rosa Parks

♦ *Why not go out on a limb? That's where all the fruit is!* Mark Twain

♦ *You have to expect things of yourself before you can do them.* Michael Jordan

♦ *You must do the things you think you cannot do.* Eleanor Roosevelt

Friendship

♦ *A friend is one before whom I may think aloud.* Ralph Waldo Emerson

♦ *He was not of an age, he was for all time.*
Ben Johnson

Happiness

- *The Constitution only gives people the right to pursue happiness. You have to catch it yourself.*   Benjamin Franklin

- *Happiness and moral duty are inseparably connected.*   George Washington

- *Put something silly in the world that ain't been there before.*   Shel Silverstein

- *Some cause happiness wherever they go; others whenever they go.*   Oscar Wilde

Integrity

- *Always remember that you are absolutely unique. Just like everyone else.*   Margaret Mead

- *As I would not be a slave, so I would not be a master.*   Abraham Lincoln

- *Hate cannot drive out hate; only love can do that.*   Martin Luther King, Jr.

- *Honesty is the first chapter in the book of wisdom.*   Thomas Jefferson

- *If you judge people you have no time to love them.*   Mother Theresa

- *It does not require many words to speak the truth.*   Chief Joseph

- *The price of greatness is responsibility.*   Sir Winston Churchill

- *The soul that is within me no man can degrade.*   Frederick Douglas

- *Words are, of course, the most powerful drug used by mankind.*   Rudyard Kipling

- *You must be the change you wish to see in the world.*   Mohandas Gandhi

Success

- *If you don't like something, change it. If you can't change it, change your attitude.*   Maya Angelou

- *In the long run we only hit what we aim at.*   Henry David Thoreau

- *It's kind of fun to do the impossible!*   Walt Disney

- *The ladder of success is best climbed by stepping on the rungs of opportunity.*   Ayn Rand

- *When you get to the end of your rope, tie a knot and hang on.*   Franklin D. Roosevelt

- *Whether you can believe you can do a thing or not, you are right.*   Henry Ford

Wisdom

- *Do not dwell in the past, do not dream of the future, concentrate the mind on the present moment.*   Buddha

- *I hear and I forget. I see and I remember. I do and I understand.*   Confucius

- *I've developed a new philosophy. I only dread one day at a time.*   Charlie Brown

- *It is the mind that makes the body.*   Sojourner Truth

- *Life is a succession of lessons which must be lived to be understood.*   Helen Keller

- *Not everything that can be counted counts, and not everything that counts can be counted.*   Albert Einstein

- *Somewhere, something incredible is waiting to be known.*   Carl Sagan

- *The only true wisdom is in knowing you know nothing.*   Socrates

- *There are some things you learn best in calm, and some in storm.*   Willa Cather

Printed in the United States
by Baker & Taylor Publisher Services